I0172950

I HAVE DECIDED TO FOLLOW JESUS

Copyright 2021 by Richard I. Gold

All rights reserved. No part of this book may be reproduced or transmitted in any form or by any means, electronic or mechanical, including photocopying, or recording, or by any information storage and retrieval system without written permission from publisher or author. The only exception is brief quotations for review.

For information address:

J2B Publishing LLC
4251 Columbia Park Road
Pomfret, MD 20657
www.J2BLLC.com

Cover by Richard I. Gold

Printed and bonded in the United States of America

ISBN: 978-1-948747-93-6

I HAVE DECIDED TO FOLLOW JESUS

RICHARD I. GOLD

J2B Publishing

Also by Richard Gold
These are available on Amazon.

Many Do Not Know My Jesus
The Wishing Tree
I Bless You God
Mary's Lamb
Work is a 4-letter Word
Remember the Good Times
God's Love - Easter Poems
Life is a Trip
Free Advice
Christmas Trees and Mistletoe
Cost of the Cross
The Tree of Salvation
The Wall and Other Poems
So Much To Accomplish
My Ghost and Other Poems
Sayings For The Believer
Psalms of Praise

DEDICATION

The author wishes to thank his wife, Penelope H. Gold for her support in developing the poems and also those who reviewed the poems and made good suggestions to improve the quality of the final product.

TABLE OF CONTENTS

INTRODUCTION

This is the account of how the song I HAVE DECIDED JESUS was composed.   It is more than most of us as Christians would be willing to endure, but it is what many of the early Christians had to endure under the Roman Empire and more than many Christians have to endure in some lands where the Name of Christ is held in repute.

This account comes from "The true story behind the song is from "I have decided to follow Jesus" in the Renewal Journal" 29 November 2017.

Let us be inspired by this true account of how one man and his faith witnessed to his village and won them the message of Jesus Christ.

NOTE: At some places, the term "man" or "men" is used in the generic sense to denote the whole human race, not just man or men.   This could carry over to the term "the sons of men" which means "child" or "children".   These terms are retained because it fits into the meter of the poem.   In some poems terms like "One" are capitalized because it refers to God or Jesus. Also capitalized is the term "Way" as it refers to the original designation for Christianity.

BACKGROUND

The song I HAVE DECIDED TO FOLLOW JESUS is known as Decision Theology for it calls on us to act on our faith.   The words to this song are:

I have decided to Follow Jesus;
I have decided to Follow Jesus;
I have decided to Follow Jesus;
No turning back, no turning back.

The world behind me, the cross before me;
The world behind me, the cross before me;
The world behind me, the cross before me;
No turning back, no turning back.

Though none go with me, I still will follow;
Though none go with me, I still will follow;
Though none go with me, I still will follow;
No turning back, no turning back.

Will you decide now to follow Jesus?
Will you decide now to follow Jesus?
Will you decide now to follow Jesus?
No turning back, no turning back.

This is from an actual experience as follows: The true story behind the song 'I have decided to follow Jesus'.

'I Have Decided to Follow Jesus' is a Christian hymn origination from India.   The lyrics are based on the last words of a man in Gsro, Assam.

About 150 years ago, there was a great revival in Wales, England.   As a result of this, many missionaries came from England and Germany to north-east India to spread the Gospel.   In a region known as Assam which was comprised of hundreds of tribes who were primitive and aggressive head-hunters.   A social custom which required the male members of the community to collect as many heads as possible.   A man's strength and ability to protect his wife was assessed by the number of heads he had collected.   Therefore, a youth of marriageable age would try and collect as many heads as possible and hang them on the walls of his house.   The more heads a man had, the more eligible he was considered.

Into this hostile and aggressive communities, came a group of missionaries from the American Baptist Missions spreading the message of love, peace and hope in Jesus Christ.   Naturally, they were not welcomed. One missionary succeeded in converting a man, his wife, and two children.   This man's faith proved contagious and many villagers began to accept Christianity.

Angry, the village chief summoned all the villagers.   He then called the family who had first converted to renounce their faith in public or face execution.   Moved by the Holy Spirit, the man instantly composed a song which became famous down the years. He sang:

"I have decided to follow Jesus.
I have decided to follow Jesus.
I have decided to follow Jesus.
No turning back, no turning back."

Enraged at the refusal of the man, the chief ordered his archers to arrow down the two children. As both boys lay twitching on the floor, the chief asked, "Will you deny your faith? You have lost both your children. You will lose your wife too?"

But the man sang these words in reply:

"Though no one joins me, I still will follow.
Though no one joins me, I still will follow.
Though no one joins me, I still will follow.
No turning back, no turning back."

The chief was beside himself with fury and ordered the man's wife to also be arrowed down. In a moment she joined her two children in death. Now he asked for the last time, "I will give you one more opportunity to deny your faith and live." In the face of death the man sang the final memorable lines:

"The cross before me, the world behind me,
The cross before me, the world behind me,
The cross before me, the world behind me,
No turning back, no turning back."

He was shot dead like the rest of his family. But with their deaths, a miracle took place. The chief who had ordered the killings was moved by the faith of the man. He wondered, "Why would a man, his wife and two children die for a Man who lived in a faraway land on another continent some 2,000 years ago? There must be some remarkable power behind the family's faith, and I too want to taste that faith."

In a spontaneous confession of faith, he declared, "I too belong to Jesus Christ!" When the crowd heard this from the mouth of their chief, the whole village accepted Christ as their Lord and Savior.

The song is based on the last words of Norseng, a man from Garo tribe of Assam (now Meghalaya and some in Assam), India. It is today the song of the Garo People.

I HAVE DECIDED

I have decided to follow Jesus
The only Son of the Most High
Who has given me the Way
To God's throne draw nigh

We have many tests in life
But the most difficult one
Is to follow as a servant
When our Christian life has begun

Let me not look away from the path
That the Holy Son has told
For it is the very best
With an end more desirable than gold

Given by the Son of the Most High
I will follow, follow the Way
To be ever right
To know what to do and say

TO KNOW THE WAY

Many years ago lived my Lord
Who came to teach and save
It was by His words and deeds
The Way of Life He gave

Would I could talk with Him
To know the way I should go
But I am given the Way of Life
This is what the Bible makes so

Perfect I will never be
But I must ever try
There are things of right
That I can never know why

But let me do my best
To be the person I should
For it is the will of God
That I do what He would

I WALK A DARK AND LONESOME WAY

I walk a dark and lonesome way
As I make my way through life
I always walk alone
It seems my way is full of strife

There is no one else who knows
What ere I have had to do
Much may not be right
I only pray that most is true

Let the way of my future
Be the way of God's Son
May it be to others and God
The new Way I have begun

So let my thoughts be ever right
Let my words and actions show
For this is the will of God
That I strive to better know

I THANK THE MOST HIGH

I thank the Most High
For the blessings I now possess
It is for the good that I must give
Thanks forever I humbly express

When I was born, I had nothing
Only the love of my mother
That was more valuable to me
Than given by another

Sometimes it seemed hard
For the life that I had to lead
But it was to her loving arms
I could always my case plead

So I will forever give thanks
For the love of family and God
This is my life today
For all my blessings I am awed

WHERE ARE YOU GOING

Where are you going
When you go out the door
Do you follow the way of right
Or do you do what is more

Do not let the right leave you
You will live a long life
Remember who you are
Remember your family and wife

So when the future comes
And you must give an account
For your words and actions
You must have a defense to mount

So what is your anchor
You fasten your life to
For every day that passes
Doing right will always be true

THOUGH NONE GO WITH ME

Though none go with me
I still will follow
Follow the way of the Lord
Follow into His hollow

I do not know what the future brings
I can but go in faith
For by the by and in the end
It will be His eternal grace

There is no other way
Given to the children of men
To be made right with God
It is the Son's truth in the end

I know the will of the Most High
To guide me in all I do
It is His everlasting light
That makes my life good and true

MY CROSS I'LL CARRY

My cross I'll carry
Though it be beyond my limit
When I walk the lonesome valley
My heart and soul in it

There is no hope for others
Except by the will of The Lord
There is forgiveness through Christ
Of which the people should not ignore
Is for the human the best

So let me know the way of life
The way of truth
For all mankind
From the time of my youth

Go tell the truth on the mountain
Go tell it to all the earth
That by the will of God
All may find their spiritual birth

LIFE IS A LONESOME VALLEY

When trials came to Jesus
He had to stand alone
He did not have us with Him
For our sins to atone

His trials were more than I could stand
To be despised and rejected
He was punished for my sins
So that my soul may be resurrected

When trials come to me
Let me remember my Lord
Who bled and died for me
Who gave me the eternal word

As He was killed that day
And raised by God in exaltation
He let me know there is a path
For my redemption and salvation

LIFE IS LONG TIME

We live from day to day
We should follow in God's way
For He has given us a comforter
To go with us each day

God is the maker of all life
The one who sustains our every breath
Let us never forget this truth
God is in charge from birth to death

God has so loved us
Loved our body and soul
That we must always know
His love will make us whole

So let us praise the Lord
Praise His Holy Name
For from eternity to eternity
He is ever the same

SOME WILL NOT FOLLOW

When they hear the truth
Some will not follow
Some will not come
Their lives and souls are hollow

But some will come when it is time
They will commit their life to the Lord
For their soul is open to the truth
They will follow the Holy Word

Some think that the truth is good
Although they will not come now
But when they finally do decide
They may find they don't know how

So wisely select the path
That leads to the Holy Will
To discover the Holy Truth
For your eternity to seal

LIFE GOES ON AND ON

Our life goes on and on
We think we have forever more
That there is always tomorrow
When we will settle our heavenly score

Then we realize that the end will come
It may come at any time
It may be after illness
It may be when we are in our prime

If we could choose how and when we will die
When we will be no more and free of debts
We could fully complete my work
And satisfy our life's regrets

We walk along the path of life
We do not know the end
But we can be very sure
That we cannot begin again

BONDING TO GOD

When we truly become a Christian
With a holy bond of love
We commit our self to God
And take our instructions from above

There is a promise from God
That comforts our needy soul
When we truly believe
It will make our eternity whole

If we believe in the will of God
If we follow His Holy Son
We will find that our eternal journey
Will have, indeed, just begun

So pray to the Holy Father
The Father of the souls of men
That He will be with us always
Until we come to life's end

BEING A CHRISTIAN

Being a Christian can seem a lonely time
When you truly feel you must obey
You may feel at times you are all alone
Following Christ is still your best way

Your God is a Holy God
Who will never leave you
He only asks that you follow
That you be ever true

So you must love the Lord
Love the Lord with all our heart
So that you may prove to be His
To follow until the time you depart

So Love the Lord
Love and follow His Son
For you may truly know
Eternity for you has just begun

GOD'S LOVE

By the love of God
He sent His only Son
To teach us what He had said
To follow the will of the Holy One

There is no other reason for this
Than the Love of the Most High
Than to show us His love
So to His truth we may draw nigh

There is no other way
To pluck the heart strings of man
Than to send the One we can identify
As God's Son Who was an exemplary Man

So let us praise the Lord
Praise Him for all His love
That in this life and the next
We will be deemed acceptable to Him above

MY WAY

My way is to do whatever I like
To walk my own way
For loss and profit each day
To do whatever comes what may

I cannot know everything of God
I can but follow my own path
And believe that it is all right
I shall not suffer eternal wrath

I must always strive to do my best
To find when I cross the great divide
I shall have peace and hope
When I am on the other side

So even when I would be tempted to do otherwise
I must walk in the straight way
So I may be made right with God
And shall be blessed on that final day

WHAT DO YOU WANT

What do you want from life
As you walk along life's way
What changes are you willing to make
As you go from day to day

God has an agenda for us
For us and all mankind
We must follow His agenda
So our actions may be aligned

So set your life's goals
Set it for your end
If you wish to be successful
Follow it carefully when you begin

The Will know of God may not always be clear
If it is His Will you wish to seek
Study and pray to find your way
In your heart you will hear Him speak

THE CROSS BEFORE ME

The world behind us, the cross before us
If we are the Holy Christian
We must be able to see
The way that our new life begin

There is only one way to God
The straight and narrow to know
We must follow this way
That all Christian must go

So pray, pray to know the Way of God
When we try to find the way to go
It will be the word of God
That we will truly know

We cannot know all things
Of what wrong paths some men will bring
But the good and perfect path
Will make the angels sing

I STILL WILL FOLLOW

Though none go with me, I still will follow
The way of the Lord is all for me
He leads me to heaven above
The Holy One to see

This way is the way of light
It leads to a better life
Though you may think of lesser
It is my rescue for eternal strife

So let us go together to the feet of God
Following the Way of the right
It will give to us from above
The everlasting Holy Light

I cannot know what it is to wander
From the path I must trod
For by the will of the Most High
It leads to the feet of God

CAN YOU KNOW THE WAY

Can you know the way
To live a good and righteous life
Always following the path of good
To keep from eternal strife

There is no other way to live
But by the teachings of Jesus Christ
If we truly know the right Way
It will pay for us the eternal price

Comfort and help the helpless
To live another day
This is the assistance we must give
And the price we must pay

Give now the price of life
To those who have not enough
To eat and to live
If it were us, it would be rough

GIVE TO THE HOLY LORD

Give to the Holy Lord
What He is truly due
He is our maker and teacher
He is just and true

No other one on earth
That is known to the children of men
Who so cares for our needs
Taught us how to begin

So know the way of the Lord
Known by men of old
Who came and told us the Way
The teachings and truths to behold

Here I am Lord
To know and follow Your Way
To do what you will have me do
Your Will to convey

FOR THOSE WHO BELIEVE

For those who have believed and died
For those who have trusted the Lord
I set my life on the holy course
To live by His Holy Word

The past is written in eternity
The present is written in light
The future is written in the Holy Word
It is by God's Holy Might

So let us truly believe in the Holy Lord
Be attuned to the will from above
Let us live the life of a saint
And spread His Word and His love

Let us pray to the Lord
To give us strength to persist
To always do His Holy Will
That all evil we may resist

LET ME HOLD TO THE RIGHT

Let me hold to the right
Never attuned to the wrong
If ever I do what I know is bad
Help me try to be strong

It is not just that I know the way
That I must forever live
If I cross from right to wrong
I must ask God to forgive

The right way is given by God
In His Holy Book
Study and pray for my good
I can find it when I look

I cannot always do right
Temptations are very strong
To do what is easy but not right
To be persuaded by the wrong

I pray for strength
To know and do the right
I ask God above
For His Holy Might

THE END OF RIGHT ON EARTH

The end of right on earth
There are powers which make it go
Powers of word, action and ideas
Attempt to make it so

But I must trust the Lord above
To help guide my mouth and hand
That I do not depart from the right
But to keep faith in God's plan

Temptations are a fork in the road of life
Which we can take either left or right
It takes a saint to choose the best
To live by God's Holy Light

So pray and meditate
On the path of God
For when the end comes
We all will be beneath the sod

THE WILL OF THE MOST HIGH

When we walk along the path of life
When we live from day to day
We are given many opportunities
To do things but not know the way

The way from our Holy Lord
The One in the sky
He knows all things that are
He understands the reason why

We cannot know all He does know
We can but try to know the Way
To live the best we can
To know what to do and say

So let our path be with the Will of God
Let us find the path of life to trod
That leads to the way above
To the very feet of our God

LIFE IS A LONELY JOURNEY

Life is a lonely journey
We walk along the way
We are responsible for all we do
We must guard what we say

For once an action is done
There is no undoing
If it is good, we will prosper
If it is evil, we are losing

What we do and say
Is what we are today
If it is good, it is well
If it is bad, we will have to pay

Let us be guided by the just
By what we know is right
Let us know God above
Let us be settled in His Might

DO YOU KNOW MY GOD?

Do you know my God?
The maker of heaven and earth
The One who always knew me
From the moment of my birth

He has a plan for each of us
Which we must study and find
A way to live on earth
To be supportive and kind

We do not always act according to His plan
We can walk our life in many ways
But to truly be successful and happy
We must walk with Him all our days

So pray for the will of the Most High
To be shown in our life
Always follow in His path
It will save us from eternal strife

HELP OF THE HELPLESS

God is the support of us all
The One who knows all our ways
He will set before us help
Be with us all our days

He fed His people in the wilderness
He showed them the way they must go
They walked with His direction
Were kept safe from every foe

Today He sets the path for us
To travel both in life and death
He will be with us always
Until we take our last breath

We worship Him in gladness
Worship as our eternal King
To His majesty and goodness
May we forever sing

GOD IS THE LORD OF LIFE

The life we lead on earth
From our birth
Is the providence of our Lord
Who shows us our worth

We may not think much of ourselves
The things we have not achieved
But God will let us know
Our worth is greater than believed

When we are on this earth
God has given us a job to do
To this end and in this way
We must be ever true

So work in the right way
From sun to when daylight turned
Because when the end comes
Our rest has been justly earned

WHAT WE DECIDE

"I have decided to follow Jesus"
Were the words of a man
Who was killed for his faith
But through his actions, his heavenly time begun

He lived in a land far away
From this place and time
But what he said and what he did
Was more than our prime

He was told that if he did not renounce Jesus
He and his family would die
But he said "I have decided to follow Jesus"
Those present wondered "Why"

He and his family did die for God
His death was an unsettling truth
That those who killed him
Found that his death was of some use

So when we think that our faith has faltered
From the way of the just
We should always remember
On Whom we placed our trust

TO WHAT END ARE YOU

When we reach the end of life
What will we have done
That our life will be remembered
What good work have we begun

We work as we live from day to day
We do not know our affect
That we may have had on others
As we strive to make a positive effect

So let us work from day to day
Let us know what we should say and do
For it is the way we live our life
That makes our influence true

May God bless our work
May God bless our life
For when we live and when we work
Our actions should avoid eternal strife

COME AND GO WITH ME

I will follow Jesus always
Will you come and go with me
Through life's snares and trials
It will be His goodness I see

Though there are temptations
I must face alone
I know that in the end
I will be in my heavenly home

God has given me His grace
Has given me assurance of His love
That after my life here on earth
I am headed to my home above

So it is with Jesus as my guide
By His Holy Word and Love
That I may be made right with God
As I travel my heavenly life above

THE HILLS OF GOD

Look to the hills of God
From whence comes our salvation
The salvation for evermore
That will give to us excitation

Let us walk the path of the Most High
Let us know His Holy Way
So that by His love
We will not for our evil have to pay

The way we must live
Is given by His holy Word
To all of us
From within the scriptures heard

Keep His Holy Word
Keep it in your heart
That you may learn how to live
And do it from the start

TO GOD BE THE GLORY

To God be the glory
Great things He has done
So loved us all
He sent us His Son

His Son came to save us
From this world of sin
Came to teach us
How to begin

As God so loved us
We must love and obey
For His Son came to us
Our sin debt to pay

Rejoice, rejoice for His love
Rejoice every day
To our fellow believers
This is what you must say

LET NO ONE DESPISE

Let no one despise your faith
But follow our Lord
For He has given us His Word
As our spirits soared

Keep the faith in the Father
Through Jesus Christ His Son
That in this life and the next
When eternity we will have won

March, march to the steps of the Lord
March and make it your way
That you may live as you ought
Teach your tongue to know what to say

It is but a short time
We have on this earth
But we must remember always
Christ gave us the Holy Birth

THE LORD OF LIFE

When we walk with the Lord
We begin to better know the Lord
Who has made the world
Who deserves to be adored

How can we know our Holy God
Who is the Lord of Life
Who came to save us
From a world of strife

We should seek an understanding
Of His Holy Name
That we find of Him
From age to age the same

So we must worship His Holy Name
We must worship in humble adoration
For we will find when we worship
The way to eternal salvation

WHAT SHALL I GIVE TO GOD

What shall I give to God
Not my wealth, not my possessions
What do I have that He desires
But to have me to confess my transgressions

God has the whole world
Has it in every part
So what I have seems minor
I shall give Him my heart

I shall dedicate my life
To His Holy Will
That in all things
My duty I can fulfill

I shall love the Lord my God
By all I say and do
I shall show it is so
Then others will know it too

SERVE THE LORD WITH GLADNESS

Serve the Lord with gladness
Serve Him with praise
We will be faithful to His Word
All our days

Serve the Lord with love
Go His way and follow His word
Let us know what we should do
To bring praises to the Lord

There is no way we may go
That is not in the will of the Lord
For if we know His Way
It is His Holy Word

So I will follow His will
From day to day
That I may please Him
In all I do and say

THE TIME TO WORSHIP THE LORD

When is the time to worship the Lord
The maker of heaven and earth
That by His will and by His power
All things were given birth

We cannot truly understand
The will of the Most High
Except by His Will and Love
He lets us know why

So worship, worship the Lord
Worship Him by day and night
That you find what you should do
To serve the Lord and do what is right

Love the Lord, love Him in every way
That you may always do right
You will be pleasing to Him
Guided by His holy Light

LIFE MAY BE A LONESOME WAY

Life may be a lonesome way
When we seek the Lord
But this is a holy Way
When we seek His word

It has always been so
It will forever be
That when we know the truth
It will be heaven's gate we see

To enter into Heaven
Will be by the will of God
There is no other way
When we are beneath the sod

So praise the Lord
Follow in His way
Let Him guide your life
To know what to do and say

WE LIVE IN A WORLD OF TOIL AND SIN

We live in a world or toil and sin
Where it seems that the good is lost
Where we strive to do right
Success is hard at the most

No one can know the mind of God
No one can see His face
For He is above us in every way
But we depend upon His grace

Love the Lord, love His Holy Word
Live as you know you should
Always be guided by His Holiness
Do what you know is good

So work for your salvation
Salvation is only from God
That you may have it freely
When given His Holy Nod

GOD IS LOVE

The God of my salvation
Is the God of love
Who sent His only Son
From heaven above

He came in love
To teach us the Way
So that on our last day
For our sins we will not have to pay

He came as a man
Who lived and died for us
For this we owe our souls
In His example we can trust

He is coming back
This time in power
It will be at the end of time
And this will be our finest hour

TO WHAT ARE YOU COMMITTED

When going through this world
This world of toil and sin
To what are you committed
Where do you start to begin

Gird up your spirit to the cause
Do not let it go astray
For the message of Christ
Is the only true way

Consider the end you desire
Consider what you will do
Make very sure along the way
That what you do will be true

As you go along in life consider
What you are committed to
So that it will guide your life
And always bring pride to you

THE WAY TO HEAVEN

Once a young man asked Jesus
"What must I do to be saved
Can I follow in your way?"
This was the answer Jesus gave

"Follow the commandments of the Law
Do what you know is just and right"
This the young man followed always
To be acceptable in God's sight

The man said to Jesus
"This have I always done
I follow in the law of God
What must I do to have Heaven won"

"Is there more must I do
To truly be on the path?
Is there anything more
To avoid God's eternal wrath?"

Jesus said to this seeker
"Sell all you have and give to the poor"
With this the man could not obey
For then he would never need anything more

BLESS THE LITTLE CHILDREN

Once when Jesus was teaching
People brought Him their children
To be blessed and taught
The lesson was to us given

His disciples thought that this was not right
That Jesus should have taught
What the adults should do
Adults should be first they thought

But Jesus said that the children
Had a faith that was honest and pure
That their faith was what we should have
A trusting spirit that would endure

So let us learn from this
That we must always be faithful
To follow in adoration
For His love always be grateful

I WILL ARISE AND GO TO JESUS

I will arise and go to Jesus
He will give me His love and hope
That all my troubles will disappear
So I can use my faith to better cope

There is no other way
For me to be made whole
But to rest in His love
The refreshing of my soul

So I will give myself
To the Lord above
To know His caring
And His eternal love

No one on this earth
Has the power to protect
No person is everlasting so
That the protection will I get

IN THE COOL OF THE MORNING

In the cool of the morning
At the height of noon day
Comes the glory of the Lord
Who teaches us the Way

I will pray to my Lord above
I will seek Him day and night
For by His love and by His presence
He is my guiding light

There are no other ways
To be made eternally right
But by meditation and prayer
To be accepted in His sight

So I will pray to God above
I will seek His Holy Face
Meditate both day and night
Seeking His eternal grace

I CANNOT REMAIN

I cannot remain in darkness
In the grip of overpowering sin
I must go to God on high
He will show me how to begin

It seemed so pleasant
When I first did begin
Time went so very fast
But not so at the end

Now I walk a lonesome path
Through this world of toil and sin
I must make it better now
Find a better way to begin

I will pray to God above
To show me the way
That will lead to heaven above
Where I will eternally stay

I'M HERE, NOW WHERE

Along the path of life
I walk as ever I can
I think that what I see
Is the best for the children of man

But I know there is more
A better and brighter way
That in the now and in the future
Will great dividends pay

So where will I go
It will be what I need
A better future to find
To all I do plead

Come and go with me
The future to find
There is room for both of us
Come, I do not mind

I WILL FOLLOW HIM

I've found my Jesus
Follow what He says to do
I will follow Him
Follow what is kind and true

There is no end of it
When it is His will, I must go
For it is from His teachings
His love and kindness I will know

So let me know the truth
Of the will of the Most High
That we shall find peace
In the sweet by and by

May God bless us
Through Jesus Christ His Son
When as I live my life
I will be found faithful when done

THE GLORY OF GOD

The glory of God
As shown in His Holy Way
He has given us the path
Teaching us by what Jesus did say

There is no other way to live
But by the Holy Way
For if we leave the Path
Our faithfulness we will betray

For God is a God of love
A God who cares for everyone
He will show us the way to live
And how salvation is won

So love the Lord above
The Lord of all good things
It is by His hand
That salvation He brings

ABOUT THE AUTHOR

Author, Richard I. Gold has been a Christian and church member for many years. In the past 20 years, inspired by his mother's experience as a poet, he has written these poems to aid the Christian. The author was born in Bartow, Florida. He graduated from the University of South Florida, Tampa, Florida and the University of Alabama Huntsville campus, Huntsville, Alabama. He has been married for 50 years to his sweetheart who is an accomplished artist and has 2 children and 3 grandchildren.

www.ingramcontent.com/pod-product-compliance
Lightning Source LLC
Chambersburg PA
CBHW032215040426
42449CB00005B/612